UNSOLVED CRIMES

Brittany Canasi

rourkeeducationalmedia.com

Before, During, and After Reading Activities

Before Reading: Building Background Knowledge and Academic Vocabulary

"Before Reading" strategies activate prior knowledge and set a purpose for reading. Before reading a book, it is important to tap into what your child or students already know about the topic. This will help them develop their vocabulary and increase their reading comprehension.

Questions and activities to build background knowledge:
1. *Look at the cover of the book. What will this book be about?*
2. *What do you already know about the topic?*
3. *Let's study the Table of Contents. What will you learn about in the book's chapters?*
4. *What would you like to learn about this topic? Do you think you might learn about it from this book? Why or why not?*

Building Academic Vocabulary

Building academic vocabulary is critical to understanding subject content.
Assist your child or students to gain meaning of the following vocabulary words.
Content Area Vocabulary
Read the list. What do these words mean?

- *abducted*
- *alias*
- *geezer*
- *heist*
- *landscaping*
- *theories*

During Reading: Writing Component

"During Reading" strategies help to make connections, monitor understanding, generate questions, and stay focused.
1. *While reading, write in your reading journal any questions you have or anything you do not understand.*
2. *After completing each chapter, write a summary of the chapter in your reading journal.*
3. *While reading, make connections with the text and write them in your reading journal.*
   a) *Text to Self – What does this remind me of in my life? What were my feelings when I read this?*
   b) *Text to Text – What does this remind me of in another book I've read? How is this different from other books I've read?*
   c) *Text to World – What does this remind me of in the real world? Have I heard about this before? (News, current events, school, etc.…)*

After Reading: Comprehension and Extension Activity

"After Reading" strategies provide an opportunity to summarize, question, reflect, discuss, and respond to text. After reading the book, work on the following questions with your child or students to check their level of reading comprehension and content mastery.
1. How did the thieves break into Banco Central? *(Summarize)*
2. Why might some people think the Geezer Bandit has special-effects makeup skills? *(Infer)*
3. How could D.B. Cooper have survived the airplane jump? *(Asking Questions)*
4. Why do you think it's important to solve a cold case, even if it happened over a century ago? *(Text to Self Connection)*

Extension Activity
Using books or the internet, find a recently solved cold case. What methods did investigators use to solve it? Were any of those methods available at the time the crime occurred? Next, find an unsolved cold case and research current methods investigators could use to help solve it.

Table of Contents

Heists and Hijacking

Many unsolved crimes have long puzzled investigators. The trails have run cold, and the suspects are still a mystery.

These cold cases are still open, waiting to be solved.

In 1990, two people disguised as police officers stole 13 works of art from the Isabella Stewart Gardner Museum.

The art was worth more than 500 million dollars. The **heist** is the largest unsolved art theft in history.

STARK REMINDERS

Empty frames hang in the museum in place of the stolen art. This 1633 Rembrandt painting was among them.

 heist (hyest): a robbery

In 1986, thieves rode all-terrain vehicles (ATVs) through the Los Angeles storm drains. They tunneled into a bank and stole 172 thousand dollars.

The next year, they struck again. They got away with 98 thousand dollars.

TUNNEL VISION

Authorities called the thieves "the Hole in the Ground Gang."

In 1971, a man known only by the **alias** D.B. Cooper threatened to blow up a plane. He demanded 200 thousand dollars and four parachutes. Once his demands were met, he jumped from the plane.

DID D.B. SURVIVE?

Experts think he could not have survived the jump. But his body—and most of the money—was never recovered.

 alias (AY-lee-uhs): a false name, especially one used by a criminal

When the plane landed, passengers were released, and the ransom was delivered before the plane took off again.

A man nicknamed the **Geezer** Bandit robbed
16 California banks between 2009 and 2011.
The FBI thinks the Geezer Bandit is a man
between 60 and 70 years old.

THE GEEZER'S GAME

The bandit would enter the bank as a normal
customer. Then he'd pass a note to the bank
teller demanding money as he pulled out a gun.

 geezer (GEE-zuhr): slang for an odd, usually
older, man

Some people think the Geezer Bandit is actually a younger man with special-effects makeup skills.

In 2005, thieves dug long tunnels to enter Brazil's Banco Central. They stole 160 million Brazilian reais—equal to 69.5 million dollars at the time.

 landscaping (LAND-skape-ing): to improve the appearance of land by adding trees, plants, or other decoration

The burglars pretended to run a nearby **landscaping** business. When they took truckloads of dirt away from digging tunnels, no one found it strange.

Candy Crime

A group known as the Monster with 21 Faces terrorized Japanese candy companies in the 1980s. The culprits kidnapped the president of Glico, who later escaped. They claimed they poisoned Glico's candy.

The last known communication from the Monster with 21 Faces was August 12, 1985.

IT DIDN'T END THERE

The Monster with 21 Faces later threatened to poison the products of Morinaga & Co. More than 20 packages of poisoned candy were found in stores.

Mystery Murders

Elizabeth Short was brutally murdered in Los Angeles in 1947. No one was ever arrested, even after a person claiming to be her killer mailed her belongings to a newspaper.

CURIOUS CASE

More than 500 people have falsely confessed to Elizabeth's murder. Some were not even alive at the time it happened!

The press nicknamed Elizabeth Short "The Black Dahlia" based on a movie out at the same time.

Between 1968 and 1969 in Northern California, a serial killer called Zodiac was connected to multiple murders.

The Zodiac killer sent cryptograms, or coded word puzzles, to newspapers. The killer claimed the puzzles were clues to his identity.

This is the Zodiac speaking

I am rather unhappy because you people will not wear some nice ⊕ buttons. So I now have a little list, starting with the woeman + her baby that I gave a rather intersting ride fo- a coupple howers one evening a few months back that ended in my burning her car where I found them.

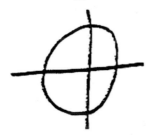

Only one of the four cryptograms the killer sent was solved.

Jack the Ripper terrorized London in 1888. No one is sure how many murders were committed by the mysterious killer.

There are more than 100 **theories** of who Jack the Ripper might have been. One suspect, George Chapman, was later hanged after poisoning three of his wives.

 theories (THEE-ur-ees): ideas or statements that explain how or why something happens

GHASTLY MURDER

IN THE EAST-END.

DREADFUL MUTILATION OF A WOMAN.

Capture : Leather Apron

Another murder of a character even more diabolical than that perpetrated in Back's Row, on Friday week, was discovered in the same neighbourhood, on Saturday morning. At about six o'clock a woman was found lying in a back yard at the foot of a passage leading to a lodging-house in a Old Brown's Lane, Spitalfields. The house is occupied by a Mrs. Richardson, who lets it out to lodgers, and the door which admits to this passage, at the foot of which lies the yard where the body was found, is always open for the convenience of lodgers. A lodger named Davis was going down to work at the time mentioned and found the woman lying on her back close to the flight of steps leading into the yard. Her throat was cut in a fearful manner. The woman's body had been completely ripped open and the heart and other organs laying about the place, and portions of the entrails round the victim's neck. An excited crowd gathered in front of Mrs. Richardson's house and also round the mortuary in old Montague Street, whither the body was quickly conveyed. As the body lies in the rough coffin in which it has been placed in the mortuary · the same coffin in which the unfortunate Mrs. Nicholls was first placed · it presents a fearful sight. The body is that of a woman about 45 years of age. The height is exactly five feet. The complexion is fair, with wavy brown hair; the eyes are blue, and two lower teeth have been knocked out. The nose is rather large and prominent.

Some people think more than one person was responsible for the killings.

The Notorious B.I.G. and Tupac were rival hip-hop artists. Both men were killed during drive-by shootings. Their murders may be related.

No suspects have been charged.

WHO DID IT?

Some theories in Tupac and Notorious
B.I.G.'s murders involve the bitter rivalry
between East and West Coast rappers, a plot
by a record executive, and the involvement
of corrupt police officers.

Victims' Victories

In 1957, two unidentified white men killed a young black man named Rogers Hamilton in Alabama. His mother witnessed the crime. Police investigated and claimed she was mistaken.

The murder is one of many unsolved civil rights era crimes against black Americans.

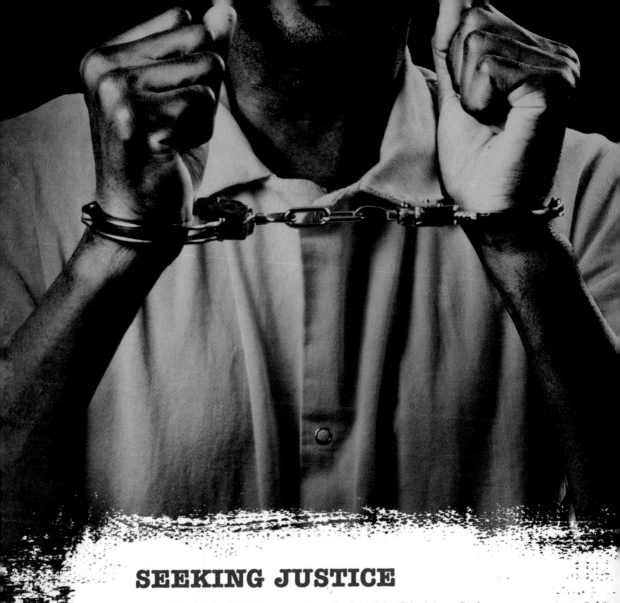

SEEKING JUSTICE

The Emmett Till Unsolved Civil Rights Crimes Reauthorization Act of 2016 is named after another unsolved murder victim. It requires the Department of Justice to report its progress on investigating unsolved civil rights era crimes.

Amber Hagerman was nine when she was **abducted** from a parking lot in 1996. Her body was found just a few miles from where she was abducted. No suspects were ever named.

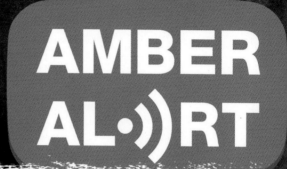

SAVING OTHERS

The AMBER Alert, a system that notifies nearby communities of missing children, was named for her.

 abducted (ab-DUHKT-id): taken away by force

More than 900 missing children have been
recovered because of AMBER Alerts.

Memory Game

Can you match the image to what you read?

Index

Show What You Know

1. What is the purpose of an AMBER Alert?

2. What is one theory behind the Tupac and Notorious B.I.G. murders?

3. What happened to Rogers Hamilton?

4. What did the Monster with 21 Faces do?

5. Who sent puzzles to newspapers?

Further Reading

Braun, Eric, *Escape from Alcatraz: The Mystery of the Three Men Who Escaped from the Rock*, Capstone Press, 2017.

Jazynka, Kitson, *History's Mysteries: Curious Clues, Cold Cases, and Puzzles from the Past*, National Geographic Children's Books, 2017.

Yasuda, Anita, *Forensics: Cool Women Who Investigate*, Nomad Press, 2016.

About the Author

Brittany Canasi's job is in cartoons, and her passion is in writing. She loves a good mystery, though she prefers the fictional kind. Brittany has a B.A. in Creative Writing from Florida State University. She lives in Los Angeles with her husband and very scruffy dogs.

Meet The Author!
www.meetREMauthors.com

© 2019 Rourke Educational Media

www.rourkeeducationalmedia.com

PHOTO CREDITS: Cover and Title Pg ©OSTILL, ©PytyCzech, ©Wiki; Pg 4-32 ©LordRunar; Pg 6, 9, 10, 12, 17, 18, 20, 28 ©ulimi; Pg 6, 10, 12, 14, 22, 28 ©marlanu; Pg 11 & 30 Wiki; Pg 17 & 30 aluxum; Pg 19 & 30 Wiki; Pg 25 & 30 caesargfx; Pg 29 & 30 gaiamoments; Pg 7 & 30 Wiki; Pg 3 OSTILL; Pg 4 LukaTDB; Pg 5 EXTREME-PHOTOGRAPHER, ilbusca; Pg 8 kamski; Pg 9 Vladimir Zapletin; Pg 10 william87; Pg 13 hobo_018; Pg 14 lucato; Pg 15 aeduard; Pg 16 Bank215; Pg 17 Svetlana Kostrykina; Pg 19 Wiki; Pg 21 Wiki, nevarpp; Pg 22 leminuit, Wiki; Pg 23 Wiki; Pg 24 trekandshoot; Pg 25 LPETTET; Pg 26 ags1973; Pg 27 Alina555; Pg 29 RapidEye

Edited by: Keli Sipperley
Cover and interior design by: Kathy Walsh

Library of Congress PCN Data

Unsolved Crimes / Brittany Canasi
(Unexplained)
 ISBN 978-1-64369-064-3 (hard cover)
 ISBN 978-1-64369-075-9 (soft cover)
 ISBN 978-1-64369-211-1 (e-Book)
Library of Congress Control Number: 2018955885

Rourke Educational Media
Printed in the United States of America,
North Mankato, Minnesota